FOOD BRANDS WE LOVE

GATORADE

By Kaitlyn Duling

Kaleidoscope
Minneapolis, MN

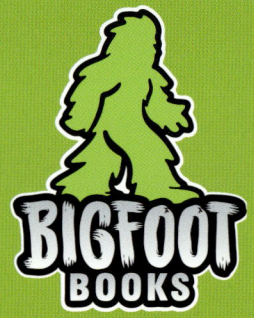

The Quest for Discovery Never Ends

....

This edition is co-published by agreement between Kaleidoscope and World Book, Inc.

Kaleidoscope Publishing, Inc.
6012 Blue Circle Drive
Minnetonka, MN 55343 U.S.A.

World Book, Inc.
180 North LaSalle St., Suite 900
Chicago IL 60601 U.S.A.

All rights reserved. No part of this book may be reproduced in any form without written permission from the publishers.

Kaleidoscope ISBNs
978-1-64519-210-7 (library bound)
978-1-64519-278-7 (ebook)

World Book ISBN
978-0-7166-4188-9 (library bound)

Library of Congress Control Number
2020936209

Text copyright © 2021 by Kaleidoscope Publishing, Inc. All-Star Sports, Bigfoot Books, and associated logos are trademarks and/or registered trademarks of Kaleidoscope Publishing, Inc.

Developed and produced by Focus Strategic Communications Inc.

Printed in the United States of America.

Bigfoot lurks within one of the images in this book. It's up to you to find him!

TABLE OF CONTENTS

Chapter 1: The Ultimate Sports Drink 4

Chapter 2: History of Gatorade 10

Chapter 3: The Science behind Gatorade 16

Chapter 4: Fueling the Future 22

Beyond the Book 28
Research Ninja 29
Further Resources 30
Glossary 31
Index 32
Photo Credits 32
About the Author 32

Chapter 1
The Ultimate Sports Drink

The buzzer sounded. The basketball swished through the net. The game was over. Sarah clapped her teammates on the back. She shook the other players' hands. Her team had won.

Sarah's face was sweaty. She tried to catch her breath. Her coach handed out cups of Gatorade. The cold, tangy liquid slid down her throat. The lemon-lime flavor was tasty and refreshing. She felt her body begin to cool down. She asked for another cup.

FUN FACT
The very first Gatorade flavor was lemon-lime.

High school basketball games can be exhausting.

The bright green Gatorade cups are a common sight at sporting events.

Many football players drink Gatorade.

Sarah loves Gatorade. She drinks it before and after games. She is not alone. Everyone on Sarah's team drinks Gatorade. High school students drink it. Young children drink it. Even **professional** athletes drink it. Gatorade is the official sports drink of the National Basketball Association (NBA) and Major League Baseball (MLB).

Gatorade is served in bottles, cups, and coolers. You can find it on golf courses. You can find it in hockey rinks. You can find it on volleyball courts. Gatorade is just one **brand** of sports drink, but it has a long history. Teams have trusted it for more than 50 years.

Hockey players can sweat out one and a half quarts of fluid during a game.

Gatorade is available in over 80 countries around the world.

After the game, Sarah got another bottle of Gatorade. This one was orange. She liked the flavor. Sarah's coach wanted her to drink Gatorade before and after games. Her team drank it at practices, too. Gatorade helps athletes stay **hydrated**. When they hydrate well, they can run faster and play longer. They can push their bodies to do more. Sometimes, they can win.

FUN FACT
Gatorade's second flavor, orange, debuted in 1969.

Gatorade Fruit Punch is popular with many athletes.

Chapter 2
History of Gatorade

Gatorade has a long and interesting history. It all started in the summer of 1965. Robert Graves, the football coach at the University of Florida, had a problem. The heat was making his players tired. Florida is very hot, even in the fall. The stadium at the university is called "The Swamp," and the name is accurate. The hot, humid weather, combined with the heavy pads players wore, were making some of the players sick. The coach asked a team of doctors to help him solve the problem.

FUN FACT
Each year, more than 100 billion ounces (3 billion L) of Gatorade are sold in the United States. That is about 142 bottles per second.

The experts went to work. They found that players were sweating a lot in the Florida heat. Football is a tough game. The players were losing **electrolytes** that provide energy. In the lab, the doctors made a drink. It was green. The drink tasted like lemonade. It was given to the football team. They were called the Gators. That is how the drink got the name Gatorade.

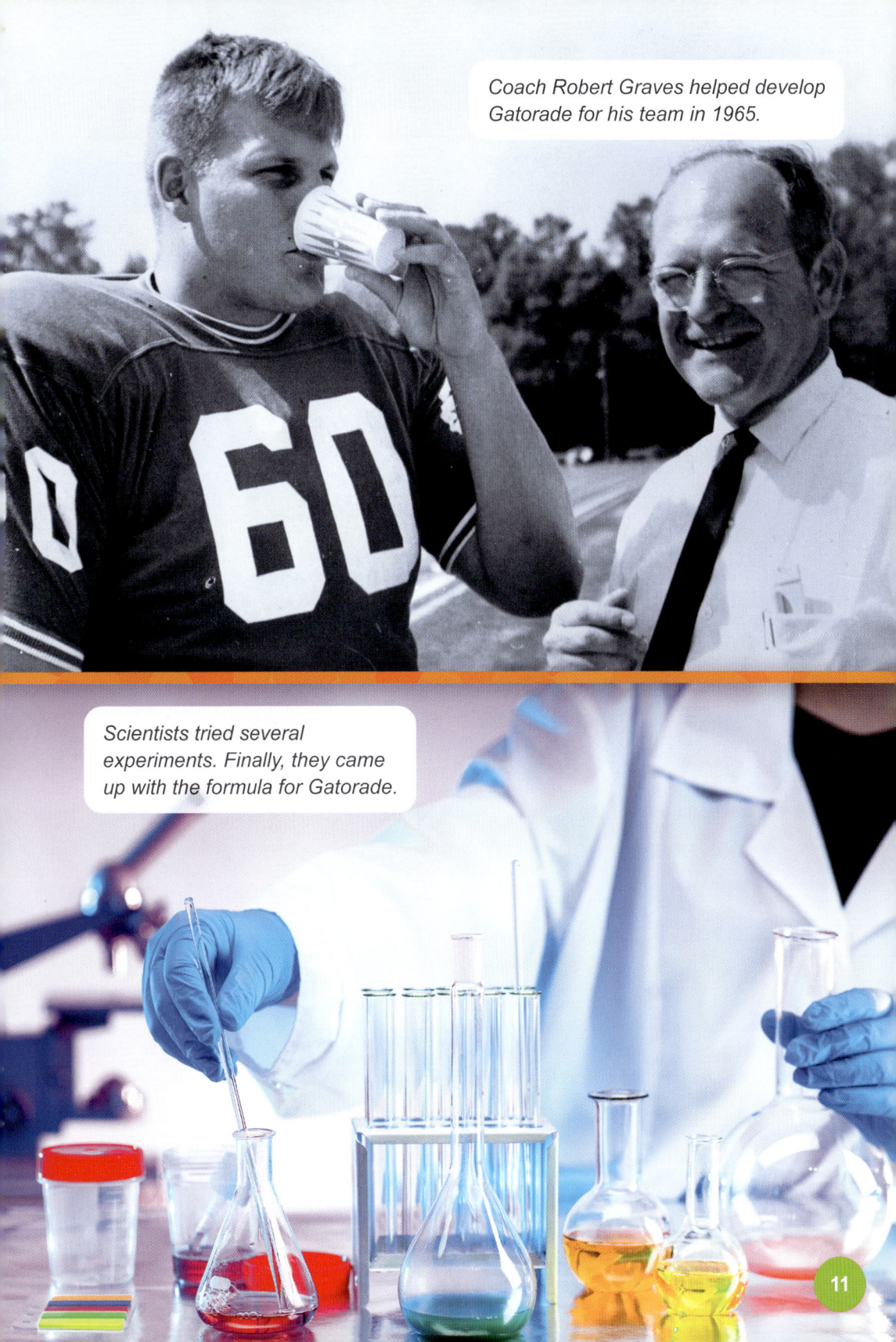

Coach Robert Graves helped develop Gatorade for his team in 1965.

Scientists tried several experiments. Finally, they came up with the formula for Gatorade.

The Florida Gators and other football teams needed a way to stay hydrated in the heat.

As the Gators drank the new Gatorade, they started winning games. They even won some big games, such as the 1967 Orange Bowl. They had more energy. They were able to push harder and run longer. Soon, word spread. Other schools ordered the drink. It became popular on college football fields.

Today, more than 70 large colleges supply their football players with Gatorade. Other sports started using it, too. It showed up on basketball courts and baseball diamonds. It even made it to the National Football League (NFL). In 1983, Gatorade became the official sports drink of the NFL. That is also the year the brand was purchased by Quaker Oats—the same company that makes oatmeal.

In those early years, Gatorade was poured from coolers into cups. Players drank it on the sidelines at games. To be sold in stores, the brand needed to bottle its drink. The first Gatorade bottles were glass. The bottle has been redesigned several times since then. In 2001, Quaker was purchased by PepsiCo. Today, Gatorade is a big part of PepsiCo's business. All along, the brand has worked hard to give athletes what they need and want.

Gatorade became the official sports drink of the NFL in 1983, 18 years after it was first developed.

GATORADE TIMELINE

1970
Gatorade appears on the Kansas City Chiefs sideline during their Super Bowl victory.

1965
Experts at the University of Florida invent Gatorade.

1983
Fruit Punch flavor debuts.

1983
Gatorade becomes the official sports drink of the NFL.

1965 1969 1970 1973 1982 1983 1985

1969
Gatorade brings out its Orange flavor.

1985
Gatorade founds the Gatorade Sports Science Institute.

1973
Gatorade introduces its bolt logo.

1982
The brand expands internationally.

1988
Coca-Cola introduces a direct competitor, Powerade.

1999
Mia Hamm becomes the first female Gatorade spokesperson.

2001
PepsiCo purchases Quaker, which owns Gatorade.

2007
Gatorade starts making the low-calorie G2 line.

1988 1991 1999 2000 2001 2007 2013

1991
Michael Jordan becomes the first Gatorade spokesperson.

2000
Gatorade introduces Propel, a flavored water.

2001
Gatorade launches nutrition shakes and energy bars.

2013
The sleek Gatorade Thirst Quencher bottle comes out.

Chapter 3
The Science behind Gatorade

Cam took a sip of Gatorade. He looked out at the field. Halftime was almost over. His team was behind. He did not want to let his teammates down. Could he score a touchdown for his team? Could they win the game? He was not so sure.

The first half of the game had left him tired. That is why he was drinking Gatorade. The September sun was hot. The players had to run up and down the field. Cam needed the **carbohydrates** that the drink provided, such as sugar. Carbohydrates give the body energy. Cam's coach blew the whistle. It was time to get back in the game.

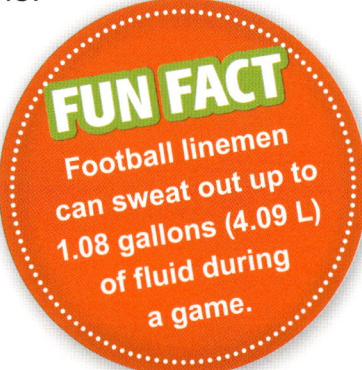

FUN FACT
Football linemen can sweat out up to 1.08 gallons (4.09 L) of fluid during a game.

High school football players need to pay close attention to hydration.

Gatorade Orange is also a favorite with Australian soccer players.

Cam took one last drink of Gatorade. His coach knew that sports drinks, such as Gatorade, could help his players. Gatorade contains sodium and potassium. Sodium is also found in salt. Potassium is found in bananas. These are both electrolytes. Gatorade helps replace any electrolytes the body loses during exercise. It helps keep the body in balance.

Cam loved the sweet taste of Gatorade. Each 20 ounce (591 ml) bottle of Gatorade has eight teaspoons (34 g) of sugar in it. When Cam joined his team on the field, he felt energized. All the sugar helped power him into the next half of the game. He kicked. He ran. He had energy. The electrolytes helped his body keep going.

ON THE FIELD AND IN THE LAB

Gatorade Sports Science Institute (GSSI) was founded in 1985. It is located in Barrington, Illinois, just outside Chicago. GSSI provides testing for athletes. It is also used to develop new and better products.

Nothing beats catching the touchdown pass and winning the game.

During the last minute of the game, Cam caught a wide pass and took off running. He pumped his legs as hard as he could, watching other players fall away. When the crowd cheered, Cam knew he had done it. His team won the game. As Cam walked off the field, he quenched his thirst with more Gatorade. It had never tasted better.

BENEFITS OF EXERCISE

Reduces Body Fat

Strengthens Muscles

Enhances Oxygen Turnover

Reduces Weight

Reduces Risk of Heart Disease

Improves Lung Function

Releases Endorphins

Boosts Metabolism

Strengthens Joints & Bones

Strengthens Immune System

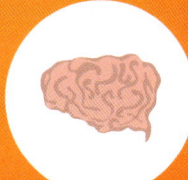
Improves Brain Function

Chapter 4
Fueling the Future

The alarm clock rang. Cory groaned. She did not want to get up, but the time had come. The race would start in just one hour. She had trained for weeks. The marathon would be long. Most marathons take four to five hours to complete. It would certainly be difficult. But it would also be worth it. As she got ready, Cory munched on a Gatorade protein bar. The brand is much bigger than just drinks.

Cory loved to drink Gatorade, but she also used the company's other products. She packed energy chews for the race course. They provide energy to **endurance** athletes. Throughout the race, there would be tables stocked with water. There would also be tables stocked with Gatorade. Cory needed to keep her body hydrated. The race course covered 26.2 miles (42.2 km).

Gatorade makes Whey Protein Bars.

Runners need to keep hydrated during marathon races.

Gatorade Fruit Punch comes in 32 ounce bottles (shown here) as well as 20 and 12 ounce bottles.

From team sports to events such as marathons, Gatorade continues to fuel athletes. Over the past few decades, the brand has grown. It now makes bars, chews, gels, drinks, and more. Protein powders help athletes build muscle.

More products are geared toward health. Gatorade even makes low-calorie, sugar-free, and **organic** drinks. In 2019, Gatorade launched its first **caffeinated** drink. It is called Bolt24 Energize.

COACHES ON ICE

The Gatorade shower has become a beloved tradition in many sports, including football. After a big win, team members dump a cooler of Gatorade on their coach's head. It is also known as the dunk or bath. It dates back to the 1980s.

Cory used the Fierce drinks in her training. They have bolder, more intense flavors. Her favorite was grape, so she put that in her bottle for the marathon. As she neared the finish line, Cory felt sweat pouring down her face. She put one foot in front of the other, pushing hard as the faces in the crowd became a blur. At this point, the time on the clock did not matter. As she crossed the finish line, Cory's face tilted up to the sky. Her smile was 26.2 miles wide.

HYDRATING ON THE RACE TRACK

In 2001, Gatorade created a special system for race car drivers. Drivers can sweat off 10 pounds in a three-hour race. Dehydration becomes a problem. The Gatorade In-Car Drink System (GIDS) holds 100 oz. of Gatorade in an insulated container. A battery operated pump delivers the liquid to the driver's mouth hands-free. It is now a standard piece of racing equipment.

Marathon races are grueling. Contestants need to stay hydrated.

BEYOND THE BOOK

After reading the book, it's time to think about what you learned. Try the following exercises to jumpstart your ideas.

THINK

THAT'S NEWS TO ME. Gatorade is always introducing new products, flavors, and ideas. Consider how you learn about new foods and brands. What information can be found in news articles? What about news programs on TV? Where can you go to find news you can trust?

CREATE

PRIMARY SOURCES. Primary sources provide firsthand accounts of an event. Interviews, videos, and photographs are all examples of primary sources. Create a list of the kinds of primary sources you might be able to find about Gatorade.

SHARE

WHAT'S YOUR OPINION? The text states that Gatorade has worked hard to give athletes what they need and want. Do you agree with that statement? Provide evidence from the text to support your opinion. Share your position and evidence with a friend. Does your friend find the argument convincing?

GROW

DRAWING CONNECTIONS. Create a diagram that shows and explains connections between exercise and the body. How does learning about the science help you better understand Gatorade?

RESEARCH NINJA

Visit www.ninjaresearcher.com/2107 to learn how to take your research skills and book report writing to the next level!

RESEARCH

DIGITAL LITERACY TOOLS

SEARCH LIKE A PRO
Learn how to use search engines to find useful websites.

FACT OR FAKE?
Discover how you can tell a trusted website from an untrustworthy resource.

TEXT DETECTIVE
Explore how to zero in on the information you need most.

SHOW YOUR WORK
Research responsibly—learn how to cite sources.

WRITE

GET TO THE POINT
Learn how to express your main ideas.

PLAN OF ATTACK
Learn prewriting exercises and create an outline.

DOWNLOADABLE REPORT FORMS

Further Resources

BOOKS

Adamson, Thomas K. *Olympic Records*. Hopkins, MN: Bellwether Media, 2018.

Green, Sara. *ESPN*. Hopkins, MN: Bellwether Media, 2018.

Hancock, James. *Leadership in Sports*. Minneapolis, MN: Jump!, 2020.

Morey, Allan. *Football Records*. Hopkins, MN: Bellwether Media, 2018.

WEBSITES

FACTSURFER

Factsurfer.com gives you a safe, fun way to find more information.

1. Go to www.factsurfer.com.
2. Enter "Gatorade" into the search box and click 🔍
3. Select your book cover to see a list of related websites.

brand: The name of a product made by a company.

caffeinated: Contains caffeine, a compound that stimulates the nervous system.

carbohydrates: Compounds, including sugars and starch, that can be broken down to release energy into the body.

electrolytes: Minerals involved in many important processes in the body.

endurance: The ability to withstand something that takes place over a long period of time and requires staying power.

hydrated: Adequately supplied with water or liquid.

organic: Made or grown without the use of chemical fertilizers or pesticides.

professional: Anyone who gets paid to do something, such as play a sport.

quencher: A substance that brings something to an end, such as satisfying one's thirst by drinking.

Index

Bolt24 Energize, 25
carbohydrates, 16
containers, 7, 13
electrolytes, 10, 18, 19
endurance, 22
exercise, 18, 21
Fierce drinks, 26
flavors, 4, 9, 14, 15, 26
Gatorade shower, 25
Gatorade Sports Science Institute, 14, 19
Graves, Robert, 10, 11
history, 10, 11, 12, 13, 14, 15
hydration: 9, 12, 17, 22, 23, 26, 27
marathons, 22, 23, 24, 25, 26, 27
running, 9, 12, 16, 20, 22, 23, 24, 25, 26, 27
science, 16, 17, 18, 19, 20, 21
sweat, 4, 7, 10, 16, 26
timeline, 14, 15
Whey Protein Bars, 22

PHOTO CREDITS

The images in this book are reproduced through the courtesy of: LunaseeStudios/Shutterstock Images, front cover (Gatorade plastic drink bottle), pp. 3, 4; NoDerog/iStockphoto, front cover (assortment of Gatorade sports drinks), pp. 1, 14 (bottom); Christopher Gardiner/Shutterstock Images, front cover (Gatorade drink crystals); Paul Orr/Shutterstock Images, front cover (water cooler); Ekkamai Chaikanta/Shutterstock Images, front cover (Gatorade logo); foxaon1987/Shutterstock Images, p. 1 (background); Monkey Business Images/Shutterstock Images, p. 5 (top); Joel Carillet/iStockphoto, p. 5 (bottom); Joe Robbins/Getty Images, p. 6; Mark Blinch/NHLI/Getty Images, p. 7; Sheila Fitzgerald/Shutterstock Images, pp. 8-9, 26; PJiiiJane/Shutterstock Images, p. 9; University of Florida/Collegiate Images/Getty Images, p. 11 (top); FOTOGRIN/Shutterstock Images, p. 11 (bottom); Gary McCullough/Cal Sport Media/AP Images, p. 12; Ken Durden/Shutterstock Images, p. 13; dean bertoncelj/Shutterstock Images, p. 14 (top); David Tonelson/Shutterstock Images, pp. 15 (top left), 24; Mihai_Andritoiu/Shutterstock Images, p. 15 (top right); Keith Homan/Shutterstock Images, p. 15 (bottom left); imwaltersy/Shutterstock Images, p. 15 (bottom right); Nagel Photography/Shutterstock Images, p. 17; Joe Giddens/PA Images/Alamy Stock Photo, p. 18 (top); Chones/Shutterstock Images, p. 18 (salt shaker); Iana Alter/Shutterstock Images, p. 18 (bananas); Sueswim03/Public Domain, p. 19; Brocreative/Shutterstock Images, p. 20; Inspiring/Shutterstock Images, p. 21; Keith Homan/Alamy Stock Photo, p. 22; wavebreakmedia/Shutterstock Images, p. 23; David Rosenblum/Icon Sportswire/AP Images, p. 25; Una Shimpraga/Shutterstock Images, pp. 26-27.

About the Author

Kaitlyn Duling uses sports drinks to help her run marathons. She has written more than 100 books for children. She lives in Washington, D.C.